God is Eternal

A children's book produced by
The Bible Tells Me So Press

Copyright © 2019
The Bible Tells Me So Corporation

All rights reserved. No part of this book, neither text nor illustrations, may be reproduced without permission in writing by the publisher.

PUBLISHED BY
THE BIBLE TELLS ME SO CORPORATION
WWW.THEBIBLETELLSMESO.COM

First Printing July, 2019

God is

eternal.

He was in the past;

He's still here right now

and ever will last.

**Before
things were made,**

**before
trees
or air,**

before time began,

God's always been there

throughout history

always will be.

Because He is God,

He'll be forever

our God and our friend.

So through all your life,

remember that God

will **always** be here.

Before the mountains
were brought forth,
and before You gave birth
to the earth and the world,
indeed from eternity to eternity,
You are God.

Psalm 90:2

For more
books, videos, songs, and crafts,
visit us online at
TheBibleTellsMeSo.com

Standing on the Bible and growing!